Church Whys and Wherefores

By

Father Edmund N. Straszak

Copyright © 2015 by Edmund N. Straszak

All rights reserved. No part of this publication may be reproduced, distributed, or transmitted in any form or by any means, including photocopying, recording, or other electronic or mechanical methods, without the prior written permission of the publisher, except in the case of brief quotations embodied in critical reviews and certain other noncommercial uses permitted by copyright law. For permission requests, write to the author, at the address below.

Father Edmund N. Straszak, All Saints' Vicarage, 89 Moor Road, Chorley, Lancs. PR7 2LR. England or email: enstraszak@gmail.com

Table of Contents

Series 1 5

  What We Do In Church, and Why 5

    1. Making The Sign of The Cross 6

    2. Anointing With Oil 10

    3. Genuflecting and Bowing 15

    4. Incense 19

    5. Lighting a Candle 23

    6. Asking The Prayers of The Saints 27

Series 2 32

  Some Church Services Explained 32

    7. The Seven Sacraments 33

    8. The Eucharist 37

    9. Holy Baptism and Confirmation 41

    10. Confession and Healing 45

    11. Ordination of Bishops and Priests 48

    12. Marriage 52

    13. Daily Offices of Prayer 56

Series 3 59

  Some Holy Week Services Explained 59

    14. Maundy or Holy Thursday 60

    15. Good Friday 63

    16. Holy Saturday 67

Series 4 71

Some Christian Ideas 71
   17. Incarnation 72
   18. Resurrection 81

Series 1

What We Do In Church, and Why

1. Making The Sign of The Cross

The Cross and Christianity.
St. Paul writes: "Far be it from me to glory except in the cross of Our Lord Jesus Christ" (Gal 6:14). For St. Paul the Cross is one of the two hinges of our faith, the other is the Resurrection. In fact, for St. Paul, Resurrection is only possible after we have been crucified "to the world" and the world to us.

This idea is at the heart of Christian belief: that Resurrection is the reward or goal, but the Cross is the means. The road to God and eternal life leads through the Cross.

How to make the sign of the Cross.
Making the sign of the cross is a feature of worship throughout Christendom, although its form varies from East to West. It can be made over other people and objects, or 'self-administered'.

In the Western Church, including the Church of England, it is usually made with the right hand. You begin by 1. touching the forehead, 2. bringing the hand down to the 'heart', 3. touching the left shoulder and then bringing the hand across the chest to the right shoulder. In one fluid action you will trace the sign of the cross upon yourself.

When to make the sign of the Cross.
The sign of the cross can be made at almost any time. It is more usually made either in response to it being traced over us, in blessing by a Priest, or at particularly significant points in worship and prayer.

During the Eucharist.
There are nine points, within the Eucharist, at which the sign of the cross is commonly made upon oneself. They are: 1. At the words, "In the name of the Father, and of the Son, and of the Holy Spirit, Amen." 2. At the words of absolution. 3. At the beginning of the Gospel reading*. 4. At the end of the prayer for the dead in the intercessions. 5. (During the Prayer of Consecration) When the Consecrated Host is raised and (6) when the Chalice is raised. 7. At Holy Communion- before receiving the Host, and 8.- before receiving the Chalice. 9. When the Priest pronounces the final blessing.

Other Times.
It will be noticed that numbers 1,2,4, and 9 also occur frequently during Morning and Evening Prayer, in the Occasional Offices, and private prayer. It is equally appropriate to make the sign of the cross at those times, and at the beginning of the Gospel Canticles: Benedictus, Magnificat, and Nunc Dimittis.

Some Churches are fortunate enough to have a small dish or bowl of 'Holy Water' (called a 'Stoup') near to the entrance. It is a good practice, when entering or leaving such a Church, to dip a finger in and make the sign of the cross with the water. This will remind you of your Baptism and Confirmation in which you were signed with the sign of the cross.

The Cross as 'Sign'.
The symbol of the cross is common to Christians of all traditions, and has been since the beginning of Christian history. It is to be seen in art, in and on our Churches, and as ornaments on our bodies. All

of this is appropriate for Christians, because the sign of the cross constantly reminds us of what Christ did for us all.

When we make the sign of the cross, we are reminding ourselves of this. We are also reminding ourselves that what Christ did on the cross 'He did for me' personally!

In making the sign of the cross, we "glory in the Cross of Christ", and we 'take-up our cross'. When we 'take-up our cross' we must be prepared to say to God 'not what I will, but your will be done'. 'Not I, but thou!'

The Cross as 'prayer'.
Very often when we make the sign of the cross, we do it to accompany another prayer. For example we make the sign of the cross when we say the words "In the name of the Father---etc". In this case the three points of the cross may remind us of the Trinity. Making the sign of the cross is also a prayer itself: a prayer without words.

It is fitting that when we come together in worship, we should worship with all our being. We are to worship with our minds, our souls, and also our bodies, for our bodies are the "Temple of the Holy Spirit". Making the sign of the cross is nothing less than worshipping with our bodies, for what is more fitting for the body than movement and gesture?

When we use words to pray, we are using only one form of language. The body has its own language also, in which making the sign of the cross is an eloquent expression. One small gesture can speak volumes of words.

(*: The way of making the sign of the cross at the beginning of the Gospel differs slightly from the usual way. It is made with the thumb of the right hand, and consists of three crosses in one. A small cross is traced on the forehead, and then on the lips, before the hand is moved to the breast. This reminds us that we are redeemed in all our parts: mind, spirit and body.)

2. Anointing With Oil

Oil As Symbol.

We are all familiar with oil, in one form or another, in all aspects of our daily lives. We use it for cooking, heating, lubricating, and in a thousand and one other ways. Without it there would be no industry, no transport, and we would have to do without many of the 'plastic' goods we take for granted.

Oil has always been the 'life-blood' of society, a fact which the Jewish people of the Old Testament were very aware of. The oil which the Jews knew, and which is still in use today, is olive oil and it is the same oil which we use in Church.

For the Jews a plentiful supply of oil, along with corn and wine, was a sign of God's favour. Oil was, and still is, a sign of God's blessing because it represents all that is best in life, God's generosity to the people He loves.

Oil In Church.

We use oil in Church in two ways: we burn it in votive lamps*, and we anoint people with it. In both cases its use can be traced back to the earliest times, and is recorded in the Old Testament and the New. The Christian Church adopted the use of oil from both Jewish and pagan practice very early in its history.

Although anointing with oil largely fell from favour in the Church of England for several hundred years, its importance has been rediscovered. It was restored to its proper place in the Sacraments of Baptism and Confirmation in the Alternative Service Book (A.S.B.) and more recently in the Rites of Common Worship. Its use in the Sacrament of Unction, or Anointing of the sick and in the Ordination of Priests, is increasingly widespread.

Sacramental Oil.

Oil as a symbol reminds us of God's boundless generosity towards us, and of His never-ending love for us. When we use it to anoint people in Church, though, it is much more than merely a symbol, or reminder. It becomes one of the channels by which God's power comes into the world, by which He blesses us with His Holy Spirit.

The oil used is essentially no different to any other olive oil, but it is made special by being set aside specially for God's purposes. God takes the ordinary things of this world, in this case olive oil, and makes them holy. He works through material things to show Himself to the world and to bring people back to Himself.

The Three Oils.

The oils used for anointing are specially blessed for this purpose by the Bishop at the Chrism Mass on Maundy Thursday, so called because one of the oils is called 'Chrism'.

There are three oils used in Church, all olive oil but named for the purpose for which they will be used. They are 1. The oil of the sick, 2. The oil of catechumens, and 3. The Holy Chrism.

1. The oil of the sick.

In the letter to St. James (ch5 v14) we read: "Is any among you sick? Let him call for the elders (Priests) of the church, and let them pray over him, anointing him with oil in the name of the Lord, and the Lord will raise him up." The rite of anointing the very sick in mind or body, those about to undergo surgery, and those nearing death, with the oil of the sick is now readily available in the Church.

This kind of anointing is itself a Sacrament and so whether physical or spiritual strength is sought, the sufferer can be confident that God will provide it in response to the prayer of faith. Requests for this Sacrament should be made to a Priest, and are increasingly welcome.

2. The oil of catechumens.

A 'catechumen' is somebody who is preparing to become a Christian, and so this oil is used to accompany the Rite of Baptism. Although its use is not enforced in Common Worship, it is both allowed and is being encouraged.

When used, anointing at Baptism is a symbol which points to the gift of the Holy Spirit, which comes to the newly baptised person as it did upon Christ at His Baptism in the Jordan. In Baptism we are "born of water and the Spirit" (John 3:5), the Holy Spirit which is the gift of Christ to His Church.

3. The Holy Chrism.

Holy Chrism is the oil used to anoint people after they have been baptized, at their Confirmation, and which is used to anoint Priests at their Ordination. It is also used in the consecration of altars and Church buildings. 'Consecration' means making holy or setting apart for God's purposes. It differs from the other two oils in that it alone is not pure olive oil. A scented balsam is mixed with the oil to make the Chrism.

Anointing also reminds us that at Baptism we are made part of the Royal Priesthood of the Church. (Our Kings and Queens are anointed at their coronation, as are many Priests at their Ordination.)

How The Oil Is Used.

The oil is always either applied using a finger or thumb, or occasionally it is poured on. When applied with a finger or thumb, it is usually applied in the form of a cross**. This is to remind us that all blessings come from the crucified Christ, the source of all healing and life for the world.

When anointing accompanies Baptism, the cross is marked in oil on the baptised person's forehead. In this way they are 'sealed' with the Holy Spirit as a reminder of Revelation ch7 v3, in which the servants of God are "sealed----upon their foreheads". In Baptism we are made servants of God.

Confirmation candidates and the sick are anointed in the same way on their foreheads, and for the same reasons. The sick are also anointed on the palms of their hands, and as the need arises the infected part of their bodies may also be anointed. In this way their prayer is acted-out.

In the Sacraments of Confirmation and Ordination the anointing is in addition to the action of 'Laying-on of Hands'. In the Sacrament of Unction the anointing with prayer is at the heart of the rite, and although accompanied by the 'Laying-on of Hands', is itself the essential element.

Conclusion.

As with all things Christian, God chooses the ordinary things of this world, and by His Grace makes them extra-special. He then uses them to make His presence felt in the world. He does this when through the Holy-water of the Font He gives new and eternal life to people. He does this supremely when He takes bread and wine at the hands of a Priest and returns them as the Body and Blood of Christ. He does this when, by the means of Holy Oils, He pours His healing and life-giving Spirit into the Church and upon Her members.

*. Votive Lamps are lights which are kept burning in Church. Usually they are fuelled by oil, although occasionally they are now electricity-powered. They are to be found hanging in the Sanctuary, near an Aumbry or wall safe which houses the Blessed Sacrament, and at the shrines of Saints.

**. See Chapter 1, Making The Sign of The Cross.

3. Genuflecting and Bowing

What is GENUFLECTION?

To GENUFLECT is to 'bow the knee': to go down on one knee. Either knee will do! It is the most profound and solemn form of bowing.

The next most solemn form of BOW is a profound bow from the waist. Finally there is the simplest form in which the head alone is inclined slightly forward and down.

Why Bother?

Prayer.
"And the Word became flesh and dwelt among us" (John 1:14). These words are at the heart of the Christian Gospel. It is only because of that one almost unbelievable fact that we can pray at all. These words also remind us of a fact that some earlier generations were inclined to forget: that the whole human person, spirit, mind and body has been 'saved'. A fact emphasised when the Risen Christ ascended, or returned, to the Father taking His human body with Him.

When we pray we offer our whole self to God, we come before the throne of the Heavenly Grace with humility. The whole self seeks to be united with God. Although prayer comes from the heart it is often expressed, rightly and naturally, through our bodies.

We pray with words. We put into words, in the best way that we can, what we want to say to God. There is much that we want to say to Him, though, that we simply cannot find words to express. Indeed, the most meaningful prayer is often completely silent, for when we stop talking to God we may listen to what He might want to say.

Midway between words and silence is 'non-verbal' communication, the language of facial expression and bodily movement. It is such a powerful language because it is almost instinctive. One gesture is often worth a thousand words, as we all know! It can express attitude and state of mind, and when it accompanies words can point-up their deeper meanings to us.

Worship.
We are all familiar with signs of reverence and honour in non-Church life. Anybody who has been in a Courtroom will have seen how the officials have to 'nod', or bow the head to the Judge or Magistrate when they pass in front of him. The same is true of people who are introduced to Her Majesty the Queen; they have to curtsey or bow.

In this way we are saying that what the person stands for, or represents, is worthy of our respect. How much more is God worthy, not only of our respect, but of the worship of our souls!

In St. Paul's letter to the Philippians (ch2 v9) we read: "Therefore God has highly exalted him and bestowed on him the name which is above every name, that at the name of Jesus every knee should bow, in heaven and on earth and under the earth".

For the person who wishes to worship the Lord with all his heart, with all his soul, with all his mind and with all his strength, worship with the body is both right and natural.

<u>When to Genuflect.</u>
When we genuflect depends partly on the tradition of the Church in which we worship. Whatever the current tradition of your Church, though, the general rule should be to reserve the most solemn

reverence, i.e. genuflection, for the most solemn times. Genuflection is peculiarly appropriate in the presence of God Himself!

If you are fortunate enough to worship in a Church in which the Body of Christ (the Blessed Sacrament) is reserved, it is right to acknowledge the Lord's Real Presence with a brief act of worship on entering and leaving the building. Normally a genuflection in the direction of the place of reservation, coupled with a turning of the mind towards Him is enough.

If you are unsure whether the Blessed Sacrament is reserved in your Church, then look for the tell-tale sign of a permanently lit lamp, red or white, near to a wall-safe or 'box' fitted to, near, or suspended above an altar. The wall-safe is called an AUMBRY, the 'box' is called a TABERNACLE or SACRAMENT HOUSE, or when suspended over an altar it is called a HANGING PYX. Alternatively you could ask if there is one of these things in your Church.

Whether the Body of Christ is reserved in your Church or not, during the Eucharist the Body and Blood of the Lord certainly comes into your Church. The Real Presence of the Lord God Himself comes among us under the appearance of bread and wine, as St. Paul's first letter to the Corinthians (ch11) reminds us. When you move from your seat to go up for Communion, remember who is waiting for you at the altar, and genuflect to adore your Lord and God. After you have received the Body and Blood of the Lord, and before you retake your seat, it is a good practice to genuflect in adoration of the Lord who is still present at the altar.

When to Bow.

Although customs vary tremendously there are several points during the Eucharist at which it is traditional to bow profoundly. 1. At the words "By the power of the Holy Spirit-----and was made man" in the Creed, in honour of the Incarnation of Our Lord. 2. For the

Dominical Words, or Words of Institution, in the Eucharistic Prayer, at which moments the bread and the wine become the Body and Blood of Christ.

More generally, it has been customary to bow the head slightly at the mention of the name of Jesus, whenever it is heard in Church. This practice not only honours the sacred name, but encourages us to be attentive at all times during Divine Service.

Equally traditional is the practice of turning to the High Altar and bowing the head as you pass in front of it, honouring the throne of God in Church, the Holy of Holies.

Practice does vary so much that there can be no hard and fast rules about when to bow, or even how to bow. For many people, unused to bowing, the slightest nod of the head can feel like a tremendous movement. You may also feel very conspicuous! Don't let that put you off though because, however it feels, it is very unlikely that anybody else will notice, and you will soon become accustomed.

Above all, if you put your soul, your mind, and your body into worship you can't go far wrong.

4. Incense

What is INCENSE?
Incense is made from various aromatic resins and gums taken from trees and other plants. When burned it gives-off scented smoke. In church it is normally burned in a CENSER or THURIBLE. Because it is difficult to burn on its own, and to create the maximum amount of smoke, it is burned along with charcoal.

Which Churches Use Incense?
Most of Christianity use, of have used, incense in worship. All the Eastern Orthodox Churches burn incense at most of their services, or liturgies. In the 'west' the Roman Catholic Church burns incense at many of its services.

The Church of England used incense throughout its history, until the mid 1600's, when it fell into disuse generally. From that time, though, it continued to be used in worship in isolated churches such as York Minster, and since the mid 19th century its use has spread and increased. Nowadays many churches are rediscovering the benefits to be gained from burning incense as part of their worship.

Why Burn Incense?

Incense and Liturgy.
LITURGY is the formal and public worship of the Church, its work. The Liturgy of the Church is made-up of the liturgy of each individual Christian, and should be the best that we can possibly offer to God.

Christian worship erupts out of our love of God and our desire to express that love. As such we should worship Him with 'all our heart, with all our soul, with all our mind, and with all our strength.' Good liturgy is designed to stimulate just such a response in us, by exciting the senses and feeding our imagination.

One of the elements of good liturgy is, for example, the use of colour and movement provided by the use of colourful vestments, processions and the like. Singing and chanting is another important element of liturgy, stimulating as it does the sense of hearing. The use of incense enables even fuller participation in the liturgy by stimulating the sense of smell. It also provides colour, movement and sound as the thurible is swung and its chain 'chinks' and 'tinkles'.

Incense as Symbol.
Symbols help to point our minds in the direction of invisible realities, and speak to us in a language often richer than words alone. As a symbol, incense is exceptionally rich in associations. Of its many possible associations, two are particularly worthy of mention here.

1. In Matt ch2 v11 we read of the Maji bringing Frankincense (a particular type of incense) as a gift to the Christ child. In the words of that well-loved Christmass carol "Incense owns a Deity nigh", which means that incense is a sign of our belief in the Real Presence of Christ, the Son of God. What was good enough for the Maji is surely good enough for us!

2. In the Book of Revelation, or Apocalypse, the burning of incense appears to be an important part of the worship of heaven. In ch5 v8 we read of "golden bowls full of incense, which are the prayers of the Saints".

This whole book is symbolic, and was never intended to be taken as literally accurate. Many commentators, though, believe that the writer of the book was strongly influenced by the worship, or liturgy, of his own church. When we burn incense we remind ourselves that our prayers, like the incense, ascend to the throne of God and mingle with the prayers of the Saints in heaven.

The Offering of Incense.

At the heart of worship in the Temple at Jerusalem was sacrifice. The sacrificial offering was usually a living thing such as a lamb or bird, but the fruits of the earth were also offered, including incense. In the Temple there was even an altar specially set aside for the burning of incense.

With the destruction of the Temple by the Romans in A.D.70 the sacrificial worship of the Old Testament came to an end. The necessity for much of it had already been brought to an end, several years before, by the all-sufficient sacrifice of Christ on the Cross. Our human need to offer thanksgiving and sacrifice to God remains, however.

In our daily lives, Christians have the opportunity to give the best of themselves back to God in the service of each other. In our worship we have the opportunity to offer tokens which represent ourselves. Incense is a token of the best that we have to offer. In 2 Cor ch2 v15 we read "We are indeed the incense offered by Christ to God both for those who are on the way to salvation, and for those who are on the way to perdition: to the latter it is a deadly fume that kills, to the former a vital fragrance that brings life" (NEB).

In the Eucharistic Sacrifice we join our offering with that of Christ Himself on the cross, as at the hands of the Priest He offers Himself to the Father on our behalf. The burning of incense in the Eucharist reminds us that Christ's sacrifice is real, and just as effective for us who are alive today as it was when He died on the cross.

When We Burn Incense.

The most natural and appropriate time to burn incense is when the Lord comes among us in Person, in the Eucharist. In the same way, if you are fortunate enough to attend a church in which the service of Benediction* is available, you will find incense burned then.

Incense is traditionally burned at particular points during Divine Service, notably during the Te Deum and Benedictus at Solemn celebrations of Mattins, and during the Magnificat at Solemn Evensong. It is occasionally used at other times also, such as at funerals, and when objects and places are blessed.

*. BENEDICTION is a particularly beautiful and moving service in which Our Lord is worshipped, present in person in the Blessed Sacrament, and in which His blessing is sought.

5. Lighting a Candle

Background.

Light is something that most people take so much for granted, that we hardly give it a second thought. Nowadays most of our houses are lit by electricity, but not so long ago people relied upon gas, oil, and candle-power for artificial light.

The need for light is fundamental. There can be no life without light. It will come as no surprise, then, to learn that images of light and darkness recur throughout the Bible.

Almost the first thing that we read in the Old Testament (Gen ch1 v2) is that in the beginning "The earth was without form and void, and darkness was upon the face of the deep." The very first action of God in creation was to say "'Let there be light'; and there was light. And God saw that the light was good"(v3).

In the New Testament too, light is a key image. The Gospel according to St. John describes Our Lord as "the light". Not the 'light' created by God, but the Creator Himself! Our Lord, too, uses the image of light to teach His disciples, when He says that we should shine as lights exposed on hilltops, and not hide our faith under buckets.

Candles In Church.

The PASCHAL or EASTER CANDLE.

A Paschal Candle can be found in most churches and is easy to identify. It could well be taller and fatter than any other candle in church, but it is certain to be the only candle to be decorated with either a transfer or by being painted. From Easter to Pentecost, or Whit Sunday, it will be in a prominent position in the Church, at its heart or in the Sanctuary near to the High Altar.

The Paschal Candle is named after the PASCH, the passion, death and resurrection of the Lord. The candle is blessed at the Easter Vigil ceremonies, and represents Christ the light of the world. The Easter Vigil includes the first Eucharist of Easter, and is a dramatic re-presentation of the mysteries of creation and redemption. It begins in total darkness, but ends in a flood of candle-lit glory!

Two of the ceremonies are of particular interest here:

1. Immediately after lighting, the Paschal Candle is carried in procession through the darkened church. As the Paschal Candle approaches the Choir, the ministers and congregation in turn light candles they are holding from the Paschal Candle, and from each other. This is a powerful image of the way in which we come to share in the living light of Christ, and also spread that light throughout the world.

2. Towards the end of the Vigil, before the Eucharist, the Paschal Candle is taken in procession to the font. There, using the candle as a symbol of Christ, waters of Baptism are blessed as the candle is plunged three times into the font. This reminds us that in Baptism we enter into the tomb of death with Christ, only to rise again with Him whose Resurrection we are about to celebrate.

After Pentecost the Paschal candle is kept in the Baptistry, near to the font, for use during Holy Baptism.

Altar Candles and Processional Lights.
The number of candles used to decorate altars can vary, but traditionally they are in combinations of two, four and six. A useful rule of thumb is that the more candles, the more important the altar is likely to be!

Side and Lady Chapel altars normally have two, or sometimes four candles (two being lit for low mass, all four only being lit on high feast days). The High Altar would have anything up to six candles, but with modern reforms and celebration facing the people, two candles are becoming standard in most churches.

The more obvious symbolism is that the altar represents the throne of God, from which the light of Christ shines upon His gathered people. You may also find it helpful to meditate upon what the number and arrangement of the candles might suggest.

Candles carried in procession are a simple, but effective way of honouring both the cross which they accompany, and also the Priest as he represents the person of Christ. Their use adds both dignity and colour to the Church's worship.

Baptism Candles.
The Common Worship Rite of Baptism now provides for the presentation of a lighted candle to the newly baptised person.

Before the service begins the Paschal Candle should be lit, and the baptismal candle is lit from this. The symbolism demonstrates clearly that, through the Rite of Baptism, the newly-baptised person shares in the life of the Risen Lord, represented by the Paschal Candle. The words which accompany the candle also point to another important meaning: "This is to show that you have passed from darkness to light. Shine as a light in the world to the glory of God the Father."

Prayer Candles.
You may be fortunate enough to worship in a church which has a PRICKET STAND, or stand for holding VOTIVE or prayer candles.

If you do, or when you go into a church which does, one will usually be found near a statue/shrine of a Saint or near to the Reserved Sacrament. Lighting a candle in prayer is a powerful symbol, full of meanings. Here are some helpful ideas:

1. The lit candle reminds us of our Baptism, and the way that we share in the life of Christ by sharing in the life of the Church.

2. When we go, leaving the burning candle behind, we are reminded that our souls never leave the presence of God, in company with His Saints.

3. Prayer is not self-centred, it is God-centred, and an important element is prayer for other people and causes. When lighting your candles, it is a very good idea to light a candle for those others you want to pray for.

The candle will not be a substitute for the prayer of your heart, but an accompaniment. A small offering which, in honouring the Saint and giving glory to God, speaks both from the heart and to the heart.

Lighting votive candles in church, when asking the prayers of the Saints and thereby to the greater glory of God, is growing in popularity in the Church of England. It is a devotional practice in which many millions of Christians the world over have found inspiration.

6. Asking The Prayers of The Saints

Who are the Saints?

The word SAINT means 'holy one', and so the saints are God's holy people. In this broadest sense, all members of the Church are, potentially at least, 'saints'. St. Paul uses the word in this way in his letters, but it wasn't long before the word came to have a more specific meaning.

Very early in the life of the Church it came to be recognised that certain individuals lived more obviously 'holy' lives, or were specially favoured by God. Chief among them were those who had died for the Faith- the martyrs, and supremely the Mary the Mother of God (Jesus) herself.

As time passed the Church began to realise that holiness only sometimes went hand-in-hand with martyrdom. More often than not holiness was apparent in other, less dramatic ways. Often, though, it was only recognised after the Saint's death.

"I believe in the Communion of Saints."

Members of the Church of England say these words at least every Sunday during Morning and Evening Prayer; they are part of the Apostles' Creed. They remind us that the Church is much bigger than our own congregation, or even the entire 'Church Militant' here on Earth. They remind us that the larger part of the Church exists on the other side of the grave, the Church Expectant and the Church Triumphant.

The whole of the Church, living and departed, is united in the one eternal Eucharist. We are united to Christ by Baptism and by eating His Body and Blood in the Eucharist, and so we are intimately united to each other.

Church Expectant.

The Church Expectant consists of those Christians who have died relatively recently but who, because of their need for preparation, are unable yet to enjoy the full presence of God. We pray for those souls in the belief that our prayers, together with those of the Saints in heaven, will hasten and ease their passage. As 2 Maccabees ch.2 v.44 & 45 put it, to "pray for the dead-- (will)--free the dead from their sin" and is an altogether fine and noble act! (NEB).

Church Triumphant.

The Church Triumphant is the Church in 'heaven' and consists of the souls of all those Christians who are enjoying, to the full, the Heavenly Banquet. The Book of Revelation, although it should not be taken as literally descriptive, paints a picture of the glory of heaven and the fulfilment of the Saints. It also reminds us that the Saints in heaven continue to offer prayer to God.

Praying for ourselves and others.

Praying for the needs of other people, and for ourselves, is one of the four basic ways of praying. It is called SUPPLICATION.

We pray for ourselves, in the belief that whatever we ask in the name of Christ, God will give us. We must always remember, though, that God already knows our needs, and will provide them without waiting to be asked.

Praying for others, in particular, is one of the ways in which we demonstrate our care for them. We also ask other people to pray for us. Prayer for each other is the basic expression Christian love.

God wants us to pray in this way, not because He will only give us what we need if we ask for it, but because prayer is good for us! It helps us to be aware of God's love for us; it helps us to be aware of the needs of others, and teaches us to love them; and above all it keeps us aware of our total dependence upon Him.

Asking the prayers of the Saints.

The practice of asking the Saints to pray for us was, for many years, frowned upon as something alien to the spirit of the Church of England, and somehow wrong. Thankfully, in recent years its value has been rediscovered, and the practice is becoming more widely understood and used.

Why we ask the Saints to pray for us.

The most important reason is that God wants us to! When we ask the Saints to pray for us we are doing no more than God's will.

In their lives, many of the Saints were able, by their prayers, to bring about spectacular works of healing and other 'miracles'. Most of them, though, demonstrated that they were friends of God in more mundane ways.

Their ability to do marvellous works was not their own, but came from God. It was God's way of blessing us through them, and His way of showing us that He was honouring them; not an honour they deserved, but nonetheless God's will. The same is just as true after a Saint has died.

One of the proofs required by the Church that God wishes us to honour a person as a Saint, is that God has first honoured him/her. As a sign, God grants 'favours' in response to prayers 'addressed' through the Saint. We call these 'favours' miracles. If God gives honour, then who are we to withhold our respect and honour?

The second reason is that, just as we believe that the prayers of a 'holy' living Christian will avail for us, so will the prayers of one who is even more alive! If the prayers of we, who are far from being 'holy' and far from the throne of Grace, can work miracles, how much more will the prayers of the Saints!

St. Mary The Virgin.

Of all the Saints, the queen is St. Mary, the Mother of God (Jesus). The Gospel according to St. Luke is quite clear, Our Lady, as we delight to call her, is of all women the most blessed. She, above all people, is most favoured by God who chose her to be the mother of His only-begotten Son Jesus.

Just as Our Lady is the Saint most highly honoured by God, so it is right and fitting that she should be the most highly honoured by Christ's Church. We are told, if not commanded, in Luke ch.1 v.48, that "all generations shall call me blessed" (RSV).

Of all the means of honouring Our Lady, and indeed all the Saints, open to Christians, by far the most fitting is to ask her to pray for us. Asking her to pray for us is not to take anything away from Christ's glory, but to magnify it by doing His will and honouring His Mother. The first recorded example of people asking her prayers is in the Gospel according to St. John ch.2 v.1ff: the story of the marriage at Cana in Galilee.

In it we read that the wine for the wedding feast had run-out. Some of the servants approached Our Lady and asked her to intercede for them or, as we might express it, bring their need to the attention of Jesus. This she did, telling them to do as He told them. The result, as we all know, is that the water was turned into wine, by the gallon!

St. Luke's Gospel ch.2 v.35 shows us that it is indeed God's will that Our Lady will pray for us, and that her prayers will not go unheeded. The prophet Simeon says to Our Lady that "a sword shall pierce through thine own soul; that thoughts out of many hearts may be revealed"(RV).

Our Lady's prayer for us is that of a mother for her children. When Our Lord was dying on the cross, almost His last act was to commit "the disciple whom He loved" to her maternal care. The beloved disciple's recorded response was to make a place in his home for her. The beloved disciple, who is not named, stands for all Christians, and so it is we who are committed to her care. It should also be the response of all faithful followers of Christ to make a place for His mother in their hearts.

Probably the best known prayer to Our Lady, and one which is easy to memorize is the 'Hail Mary':

Hail Mary, full of grace, the Lord is with thee. Blessed art thou among women, and blessed is the fruit of thy womb Jesus. Holy Mary, Mother of God, pray for us sinners now and at the hour of our death. Amen.

Conclusion.

Praying for others is a demonstration of our love for each other, and of our faith in God. It is just as important, though, to ask other Christians, including the Saints, to pray for us.

Series 2

Some Church Services Explained

7. The Seven Sacraments

What are 'Sacraments'?
There are seven Sacraments. The two principal Sacraments are the Mass or Eucharist, and Holy Baptism. The other five Sacraments are Unction or Healing, Ordination, Confession or Reconciliation, Confirmation, and Marriage.

The Church teaches that the Sacraments were given by Christ either before His death on the cross, or in the case of Confession after his Resurrection. The only exception is the Sacrament of Confirmation. It began as part of the Sacrament of Baptism and became detached as infant baptism became the norm.

The Two Sides.
Any child will tell you that a coin has two sides, heads and tails. A Sacrament is rather like that. Firstly there is the side facing you, that you can see. Then there is the side that you cannot see. Even though you may not be able to see the other side of the coin you believe, even know, that it must be there. If you were able to cut the coin in half, across its length and then placed the two halves face-up, you would not have two coins; you would not even have one coin, in spite of appearances!

A Sacrament is like a whole coin; there is the side one can readily see, and there is also the side that one cannot see, but must believe in. It is this side, the spiritual side, which gives the Sacrament its power. It must possess both sides, the physical side and the spiritual side, to be genuine, and the two sides are inseparable.

How?

The physical side of a sacrament can be seen, heard, touched, tasted or smelled and acts like a pointer. It points to the reality which cannot be sensed. Unlike a sign or symbol, though, what we see, hear etc. also helps to bring the hidden reality into our world. For example:

In Baptism the pouring of water accompanied by certain words does not simply show that a person has become a Christian, it makes him one.

In the Eucharist the words which the Priest speaks, Christ's own words, do not describe something which has already happened or express some pious hope, but actually cause something to happen by the power of the Holy Spirit (the change of the bread into Christ's Body and the wine into His Blood)!

In Unction the 'laying-on of hands with prayer', accompanied by anointing with Holy Oil, does not merely give emotional comfort, but always brings-about healing of the body, mind or spirit in reality, and imparts the strength of the Holy Spirit.

It is all done by the power of the Holy Spirit. The Priest stands in Christ's own shoes and so his hands become in a mysterious way Christ's hands, his voice becomes the voice of Christ, and the power which flows through him is the power of the Holy Spirit. The Priest is God's chosen instrument and is wielded by God as His tool.

It is important to remember that a Sacrament 'works', even when the people present do not understand or believe, or in the case of a baby, are too young to believe. They even 'work' if the Priest is 'unworthy' or a sinner, because it is God's power behind them, and not magic!

Why?

The purpose of the Sacraments is to provide for all the spiritual needs of the Church and the world, and every possible need is provided-for. This does not mean that God is confined to the Sacraments, or that His power can only be seen at work in the Church. It does mean that only in the Sacraments of the Church does He guarantee that his presence can be encountered directly.

Christ is present in each one of the Sacraments. The Incarnate and Risen Lord continues his work of Redemption, or saving the world and its people, each time one of the Sacraments is celebrated.

Sacramentals.

Sacramentals are things which are associated with a Sacrament, or arise from one. Often they bring-out more clearly the meaning of a Sacrament but sometimes they can be used apart from the Sacrament which gave them birth.

For example, Holy Water which is sprinkled on a person or thing to bless it reminds us of the cleansing power of Baptism and the new birth which it gives. When it is used in a Holy Water stoup*, to make the sign of the cross on entering a church, it reminds us of our own baptism.

Another example is the blessed wedding ring, which reminds us of the unbreakable bond between a man and woman which is created in the Sacrament of Marriage.

Again the Holy oil with which people are anointed at Confirmation reminds us of the anointing at Baptism and of the gift of the Holy Spirit which is given through the laying-on of hands.

Some other examples of sacramentals are: Votive or Prayer candles, Signing with the cross at Baptism, and the Kiss of Peace.

Sacramentals are themselves channels of God's Grace and power, just like the Sacraments of which they are extensions.

Effect

The Church is described as Christ's body on earth, and so it is. Christians are part of that body and need to be nurtured if they are to grow into the likeness of Christ and be perfected. The body also has to be built-up and learn to work together as a unit with a common purpose. The Sacraments have the effect of feeding Christians and also of uniting them in common worship and purpose.

* A 'stoup' is a dish or receptacle often found near the main door of a church, or at the vestry/sacristy door. It contains Holy Water for making the sign of the cross.

8. The Eucharist

What's in a name?
Of all the 'services' in Church, by far the most frequently celebrated is the Eucharist, also known as the Mass, Holy Communion, and the Lord's Supper, in different traditions. The most ancient name, however, is Eucharist which is Greek for 'Thanksgiving', whereas arguably the best is Mass since it includes all the other meanings.

Beginnings.
The Eucharist, as a celebration, was commanded by Christ on the night He was betrayed. He took some unleavened bread* and gave it to His disciples calling it His body. He also took some wine and gave that to His disciples calling it His blood. He then said: "Do this that I might be recalled", usually translated as "Do this in memory of me".

He did this within the context of a Jewish Passover meal, which was His last meal with His disciples. The Passover is the celebration of God's mighty and miraculous acts in saving the Jewish people from slavery under the Egyptians.

The next day, Good Friday, He allowed Himself to be crucified which linked His sacrifice of Himself with the Passover Lamb, and His broken body and blood in the Eucharist.

Sacrifice.
St. Paul said "as often as you eat this bread and drink the cup you proclaim the Lord's death until He comes". This means that Christ's sacrifice, or offering of Himself, is brought into our midst and is pleaded before His Father each time the Eucharist is celebrated. Christ became the sacrificial lamb to save everybody from spiritual

slavery when He allowed Himself to be crucified. In the Eucharist Christ offers the sacrifice of Himself at the hands of the Priest.

A Simple Shape.

The Eucharist can be divided roughly into four parts:

Part 1: prepares us to meet God by confessing our sins in general, or saying how sorry we are for disobeying Him. It also sets the tone for the celebration in the prayer or 'Collect' for that day.

Part 2: is called the 'Liturgy of the Word'. In it we listen to readings from the Bible, and also listen to a sermon in which the Faith is explained and applied to current circumstances.

We say what we believe as Christians in the words of the Creed, and offer prayers for other people in the Intercessions. Sometimes the 'Peace' is shared here, sometimes it is shared just before Holy Communion.

Part 3: is called the 'Liturgy of the Eucharist'. It starts with the Offertory which is when bread, usually in the form of unleavened wafers, and wine are brought to the altar.

At its heart is the great Prayer of Consecration, or Eucharistic Prayer, which begins when the Priest says or sings:

"The Lord be with you.................

"Lift up your hearts......................

"Let us give thanks to the Lord our God................"

In this prayer, which only a Priest or Bishop can say, God performs the great miracle of changing the bread into the Body of Jesus, and the wine into the Blood of Jesus.

Part 4: is when Christians eat the bread which has become the Body of Jesus, and drink the wine which has become the Blood of Jesus. It is called Holy Communion.

When everybody has received Holy Communion, or received a blessing if they are not Confirmed, the final prayers are said and the Priest gives a general blessing, and then dismisses the people.

A Miracle.

Some people believe, wrongly, that miracles are a thing of the past, and do not happen today. The wonderful thing about the Eucharist is that a miracle happens every time it is celebrated by a Catholic Priest (usually in Britain an Anglican, Roman Catholic or Eastern Orthodox). It is a miracle which cannot be seen with the eyes, which is why some people do not see it at all. It can only be seen with the heart!

In the Eucharistic Prayer the Priest repeats the words of Christ over the bread and the wine. He then raises the bread-(now become the Body of the Lord), and the cup of wine-(now become the Precious Blood of the Lord), for the people to gaze upon with their eyes and adore with their hearts.

We worship the crucified and risen Lord really present in His flesh and blood.

Preparation and thanksgiving.

Before receiving Holy Communion it is important to be properly prepared. Since at The Eucharist we are to be guests of the God of the universe, Christ Himself, we ought to fast, or refrain from eating, for at least one hour before receiving Holy Communion. It is also a good practice to make one's confession regularly, and so come to the Lord with a clear conscience and in humility.

Before the service begins we should pray quietly that we may not eat the Body and Blood of the Lord unworthily. We should humbly ask Christ to give us the benefits of His passion. After the service we ought to sit or kneel quietly offering Him thanks.

* Unleavened bread is made without yeast and so does not rise.

9. Holy Baptism and Confirmation

The Rite of Baptism is the first of the Seven Sacraments of the Church. It derives its power from the sacrifice of Christ on the cross, which is made present in the Eucharist. After Our Lord had died, a soldier pierced His side with a spear, and at once there flowed from the wound blood and water. The Church understands this to be symbolic of the two Sacraments of the Eucharist and Baptism.

In the early Church there was no separate sacrament of Confirmation, partly because the norm was for adults to be baptised, and partly because the two acts had not yet been separated. In modern rites of Baptism there is still an echo of this original unity in the anointing with Holy Oil after the baptism with water. An important part of the Rite of Confirmation also is the anointing with Holy Oil.

Elements of the Rite of Baptism: The Visible Side.

The Rite of Baptism is made-up of two layers: a layer of necessary elements, and a layer of elements which although important are not strictly necessary for the sacrament to 'work'.

The necessary elements are:

1. A genuine desire to become part of the Church, whose beliefs are expressed in the words of the Creeds and whose God is the Holy Trinity. This is made explicit in some form of assent and promise of commitment by the adult, or in the case of a child by an adult who can speak for him.

2. The pouring of water, or the immersion in water, three times, accompanied by the words "(I baptise you) in the name of the Father, and of the Son and of the Holy Spirit. Amen."

Secondary elements are:
1. In most modern rites the candidate for Baptism, is anointed with Holy Oil once or twice. The first anointing is before the Baptism with water, and is an exorcism, intended to drive out the devil. The second, in the form of a cross on the forehead, is after the baptism and represents the gift of the Holy Spirit.

2. A lighted candle is often given to the newly baptised person as a symbol of the new life which the baptised person enjoys united to Christ "the light of the world".

3. The whole liturgy is hedged-about with various prayers, and often includes a form of 'welcome' from the gathered congregation which represents the Church at large.

Some Popular Misconceptions.
1. That Baptism is little more than a 'naming' service. Of course only a name given at Baptism is properly a 'Christian' name, but this is not the purpose of the Rite.

2. That in some way Baptism is a kind of passport, or guaranteed ticket to 'heaven'. Of course a baptised child who dies will, without doubt, enter heaven. As a person grows to maturity, though, and takes responsibility for their own actions, beliefs, and way of life, they may fall away from the True Faith or deny it altogether. In that case the fact of having been baptised will not be of much help at all!

What Happens- The Spiritual Side.
Generations of children have tried to grow apple trees by planting a pip of their favourite apple, and failed! A tree may have grown in time, but it would certainly not have produced their favourite fruit.

The only way to grow a tree that would yield the desired apple is to take a twig, or cutting, from the original tree and grow it on, or propagate it. There are several ways of doing this, but the only one likely to succeed is grafting. This involves joining the cutting to a rootstock, or rump, of a tree with strong life in its sap. The sap from the rootstock then floods into the twig and enables it to grow into a full-size fruit-yielding tree.

This is what happens to a person in Baptism. He is grafted onto the Holy Vine, the Church, which is the Body of Christ. The life-sap of the Holy Vine, which is God the Holy Spirit, then flows into the newly-baptised person. The result is that, potentially at least, the baptised Christian will live as long as the tree onto which he has been grafted, which is forever!.

The difference between a cutting and a person, however, is that unlike the cutting, a human being has the ability to separate himself from the tree onto which he has been grafted!

Confirmation

Since infant baptism became the norm Confirmation has come to be administered much later in life. Normally Confirmation is administered to young people who are considered to have reached an age at which they are able to make the Baptismal promises for themselves.

Confirmation is administered by a Bishop and involves three elements, two absolutely necessary, and the third normally considered to be necessary.

Absolutely necessary elements.

As with Baptism, explicit belief in the Faith expressed in the Apostles' Creed is required, and a promise of commitment is made. Unlike Baptism, but in common with the sacraments of Ordination and Healing, the bishop 'lays' his hands on the head of the candidate. In this way the gifts of the Holy Spirit are miraculously imparted to the candidate, to strengthen and empower him.

The third element, normally considered necessary, is the anointing with Holy Oil. Together with the 'laying on of hands' this action imparts the gifts of the Holy Spirit.

10. Confession and Healing

Marry in Haste.
The word 'repentance' means turning away from our sins in sorrow, with the intention of avoiding them in future. But first it is necessary to 'own' our sins: to admit that we have sinned, and that we are to blame.

Many people behave as though they had all the time in the world to repent, putting off until tomorrow what ought to be done today. Our Lord teaches us that the day of our judgment will come "as a thief in the night", and that we do not know "either the day or the hour". In short, there is no time like the present in which to put our spiritual house in order, and to make our peace with God! The Sacrament of Confession, or Reconciliation as it is also known, is the means provided by God through which we can make our peace with Him.

Christ in His wisdom knew that even the best of His followers, like St. Peter, would stumble and fall into sin after their Baptism. The Sacrament of Confession makes available the cleansing grace of Baptism to people who sin after their Baptism.

Who Needs It?!
Many people are under the mistaken impression that Sacramental Confession is only available to Roman Catholics. In fact the Book of Common Prayer of the Church of England encourages each member of the Church of England to make a "special confession of his sins" to a Priest, in other words to make use of Sacramental Confession!.

Some people believe that the General Confession at the beginning of the Eucharist, or Morning and Evening Prayer, is an effective substitute for Sacramental Confession. It is not! It is, as the name implies, a confession of our part in the sins of the Christian community as a whole and as such is no substitute for Sacramental Confession.

Outward Appearances.

The sacrament of Confession is unusual in that there is little formal ritual. There is, however, a clear 'shape'. Normally the 'penitent', or person making their confession, will kneel next to the Priest, sometimes separated by a partition. Within sight of the penitent there will be a crucifix to remind him at what cost his forgiveness has been won. Sometimes the Sacrament is celebrated in a room with both penitent and confessor (Priest hearing the confession) both seated.

Apart from the words spoken, the only outward sign is the sign of the cross made by the confessor over the penitent at the absolution.

The Rite usually begins with the penitent invoking the Holy Trinity, "In the name of the Father, and of the Son and of the Holy Spirit. Amen." and then asking the blessing of the Priest. After he has received the Priest's blessing the penitent begins by saying how long it is since his last confession, and then continues to give a detailed account of his sins since then. When he has finished his account the penitent asks the Priest for "Penance, advice and absolution."

The Priest will respond by giving advice, and if necessary inquiring further, until he is satisfied that the confession is full and genuine, that the penitent is truly contrite, and that the penitent has a real desire to avoid committing those same sins again. He will then give the penitent a 'penance' to say, or more rarely do. The penance usually takes the form of a prayer and is intended to act as a 'thank-you' to God for the gift of His forgiveness, and as a token of reparation. Finally the Priest will pronounce the absolution while making the sign of the cross over the penitent.

A word spoken in due season, how good it is!
Although it took many centuries to assume its present form, Sacramental Confession is one of those Sacraments instituted by Christ Himself. After His resurrection Christ came to His apostles and "breathed on them, and said to them, 'receive the Holy Spirit. If you forgive the sins of any they are forgiven; if you retain the sins of any, they are retained.'" It is this very power which is wielded by the Priest in confession, with the express authority of Christ Himself.

Priests in the Church of England are, along with all Catholic Priests, entrusted with this power and authority at their ordination when the Bishop lays hands on them saying "whose sins thou dost forgive, they are forgiven; and whose sins thou dost retain, they are retained."

Reconciliation and Healing.
As Sacramental Confession brings God's healing power to bear on the soul broken and crippled by sin, so in the Sacrament of Healing God's healing power touches the body, mind and emotions.

The Epistle of St. James teaches us that when a Christian is sick he should "call for the Priests of the Church" who will "pray over him, anointing him with oil in the name of the Lord". Invariably when a sick person requests Sacramental Healing they are hoping for a 'cure'. This is not always given, for only God knows whether or not a sick person is being called to health, or to bear the cross of suffering in union with the Lord. If a miraculous cure is not granted, however, God always gives the strength and support to enable the sick person to bear their cross, if they will only accept it!

11. Ordination of Bishops and Priests

A Chosen People, A Royal Priesthood.

As a description of the Church, these words were first used to describe the Jewish people of the Old Testament. At heart they describe not only the special relationship between themselves and God, but also their special relationship with the rest of mankind. After the death and resurrection of Christ non-Jews were called by God to share that special relationship.

Although the whole of the Jewish people were the Royal Priesthood, their divinely inspired religion was provided by God with a High Priest and orders of Levites and Priests, to enable them to exercise that Royal Priesthood. The Catholic Church, which God grew out of that religion and people, has a similar pattern.

The right to become a Jewish Priest was passed from father to son, and was the sole preserve of one tribe in Israel. In the Catholic Church, of which the Church of England is part, there is no such hereditary right. A man is called to the privilege and responsibility of Priesthood as an individual, sometimes directly by God, sometimes indirectly.

Christ became the eternal High Priest when He sacrificed Himself on the altar of the cross. Before He died, however, He chose twelve men to be Apostles to continue His work and ministry, and they in turn appointed Bishops to succeed themselves, who appointed Priests and Deacons to assist them and share in their work. And so Christ, who is our heavenly High Priest, provided His Church with High-Priest-like Bishops and with orders of Deacons and sacrificial Priests, to enable the Church to exercise its Royal Priesthood.

Isambard Kingdom Brunel.
Brunel is famous for, amongst many things, building the first great bridge between England and Wales. Similarly, that is just what Priests do: build bridges, and repair them. Bishops and Priests build spiritual bridges, between heaven and earth, or more exactly maintain the bridge built by Christ the High Priest. They do this by celebrating the seven Sacraments, which form the bridge between heaven and earth, in and through which Christ continues His work on earth.

Making, or 'Ordering'.
The power to make Bishops, Priests and Deacons is God the Holy Spirit, who was given to the Church at Pentecost. Since then the authority and power to ordain has been transmitted through the Catholic Church along the line of Bishops. They do this by the laying-on of hands with prayer. At the heart of the Ordination service, then, is the action of laying-on hands with prayer.

When a man is Ordained or Consecrated a Bishop, one or more men who are already Bishops lay their hands on his head, whilst calling down the Holy Spirit, and asking God to empower the man to perform the office and work of a Bishop in the Catholic Church. When a man is ordained as a Deacon, only a Bishop lays his hands upon him in the same way.

When a man is ordained Priest, the other Priests present join with the Bishop in laying-on their hands, which symbolises their unity with the ordinand. A very ancient custom, which had fallen into disuse in the Church of England is the anointing of the new Priest's hands with Chrism*. Many Bishops are now reintroducing this wonderful sign of the Holy Spirit.

At one point during the service the ordinand is presented with a Bible, to symbolise and remind him of where his authority comes from. Also increasingly in the Church of England, when a man is made into a Priest he is also presented with other symbols of his new office: a paten and chalice, the 'tools' of his Priestcraft, used in the offering of the sacrifice of the Mass or Eucharist.

An important thing to remember is that once a man has been ordained, it can never be undone. The gift of God, once given, can never be taken away by men, even if for some very serious reason the Church finds it necessary to rescind its authority to a Priest to exercise his Priesthood.

Man or woman?

In 1992 the General Synod of the Church of England followed the lead of much of the rest of the Anglican Communion and decided that it had the authority to allow women to become Priests. In 2014 the General Synod of the Church of England took the final step along this road when it decided that it would allow women to become bishops and in 2015 the first woman, Libby Lane, was made bishop of Stockport.

The debate over whether the Church of England did indeed have the authority to act independently of the rest of the Universal or Catholic (another name for Universal) Church still rages. For many in the Church of England the arguments in favour of this innovation were, and remain, unconvincing. The rest of the Catholic Church, both in the East and in the West, also remains opposed to such a move, which they feel flies in the face of Christ's intention and will for the Church.

The result has been a split in the Church of England, with those who remain true to the historic faith and order of the Church being unable to recognise the validity of women's ordination. Hence provision was made in 1992 and again in 2014 to enable traditional Anglicans to remain within the orbit of the Church of England by having their own Bishops and Priests who take no part in the ordination of women and are themselves ordained independently of women.

* Chrism is special 'Holy' oil blessed by a Bishop during Holy Week.

12. Marriage

One plus One equals One!

The Church believes and teaches that marriage is a 'gift of God, and a means of His grace' and that the married state is the only legitimate context for an active sexual life. She believes that it is a gift to all people, Christian and non-Christian alike, for God wants people to live in blessed relationships with one another, and be happy.

She believes, though, that Christian Sacramental Marriage is the perfect expression of this state of life. Sacramental Marriage places a man and a woman in a spiritual relationship in Christ, as well as a legal and social relationship.

She also believes that the family created by a married couple is intrinsically more stable, and able to provide the best environment for the bringing-up of children. Underlying this teaching, the church believes that marriage is a permanent state, and the promises made are binding for life.

Although increasing numbers of people, for one reason or another, feel unable to accept the Church's teaching on marriage, and particularly that it is 'for life', they still come in quite large numbers to be married in Church.

There is still an almost instinctive feel that 'one plus one equals one'; that a man and a woman in marriage become something new, even 'one flesh'!

The Marriage service in Church presents the Church's teaching in a dramatic way. It gives a refreshing emphasis to the spiritual dimension, as distinct from the monetary and social dimensions, which can so easily dominate.

Making a Start.

Processions in church are always moving occasions, and few are more moving for the unchurched than the procession of a Bride into church on her wedding day. Starting at the main door, the procession wends its way to the front of the church where the Groom and Best Man wait. The Bride walks on the right of her father, or father's stand-in*. She is often preceded by the Priest, and followed by the Bridesmaids.

On reaching the front of the church the service begins with prayers and readings from the Bible, and an explanation of the service and the nature of married life. This is followed by an invitation to anyone present, including the Bride and Groom, to make public anything which might prove an obstacle to a legal marriage, for example already having a wife in a foreign port!

Public Consent.

Since everything has to be seen to be above board, and to avoid the abuse of 'shotgun weddings', the first thing that the Bride and Groom do is to give their explicit consent to the service taking place. They also declare, publicly, their intention to remain married to each other for the whole of the rest of their lives.

This is followed by the 'giving-away' of the Bride by her father *, or transfer of responsibility for her well-being. This ceremony was of particular importance in the past when wives were generally wholly dependent upon their husbands.

Solemn Vows.

Having been 'given away', the Bride and Groom join their right hands, and facing each other, by turns make their vows to each other. The vows are Solemn because they are made in the presence of

Almighty God, but they are made to each other. In other words God is asked to hold the parties to their promises.

The promise, or vow, covers all aspects of life and does not allow any excuse or reason for breaking one's side of the bargain. It is, put simply, to dedicate oneself exclusively to the happiness of the other person, without stint and whatever the cost to oneself. The only way of terminating the relationship, allowed for, is the death of one or both of the persons! For this reason, and because Christ explicitly and categorically forbade it, the Catholic Church, including much of the Church of England, does not allow the remarriage of divorcees in Church except under very special conditions.

A Sign to All.
A very ancient tradition is for the Groom to give the Bride a ring, if possible of pure gold. Traditionally the Best Man has custody of the ring until this point, when it is given to the Priest to bless. The Groom then places the ring on the third finger of the Bride's left hand (third finger as a reminder of God the Holy Trinity). It is gold as a token and symbol of all the earthly possessions of the Groom, which he is bestowing unconditionally upon his Bride. It is often customary nowadays for the Bride to give a ring, in the same way, to the Groom.

The couple are now pronounced married, and from that moment-on are man and wife. In one final symbolic action the Priest joins the right hands of the Bride and Groom and 'ties' them together with the Priestly stole he is wearing. In words he forbids anyone from causing them to separate.

There then follows the first of two blessings given by the Priest. This is the Nuptial Blessing, given specifically to the newly-weds. The second, at the end of the service, is the general blessing given to all the people present.

Prayers, Worship, and Triumphal Procession.

It is appropriate that the rest of the service is taken-up with the worship of God. This means that the first thing that the couple do together in their married life is worship God.

At the end of the service the newly-weds are required to sign the registers and Marriage Certificate, along with two witnesses. Finally the newly-weds lead the procession out of Church.

13. Daily Offices of Prayer

Punctuation Marks.

A feature of written language is the way in which it is punctuated. Without punctuation marks written language becomes little-more than gibberish, devoid of form and meaning. It is much the same with time, with the day. Most people punctuate their daily lives with particular actions performed at particular times. With many people, for example, the capital letter which begins their day is a 'T'!!!

This is equally true of our interior, spiritual, lives. An unpunctuated spiritual life can so easily be formless and meaningless. The Daily Offices, or services, of Morning and Evening Prayer, together with the Minor Offices through the day and into the night, provide this much needed structure and form.

Little and Large.

The Daily Offices differ very much from most of the other services of the Church in that they are not Sacraments. They are services of the Word only, being composed of Psalms, canticles (which are poems found elsewhere in the Bible and Christian tradition), hymns, readings, and prayers.

The two most important offices are those of Morning and Evening Prayer. They are like the hinges on which a door is hung. The day which is hung upon Morning and Evening Prayer is well balanced and in tune with God. Priests of the Church are obliged to say, or offer, these Offices every day without exception, for a Priest who does not say his prayers is a very poor Priest indeed! Lay people, too, are encouraged to join-in with the recitation of the Daily Office either with the Priest in church, or not, as is most convenient.

The Offices can be found in several readily available forms including the Book of Common Prayer (BCP); Celebrating Common Prayer (CCP); and The Divine Office (the official version of the Roman Catholic Church). Only CCP and The Divine Office provide forms for the Lesser Hours of Prayer During the Day, Compline (or Night Prayer), and The Office of Readings (which incorporates readings from the Church Fathers and other sacred writings as well as the Bible).

Angelus

The Angelus is a short prayer which sets before us the mystery of the Incarnation, and reminds us that when Jesus came in the flesh he took possession of time. It is almost all taken from the Bible, by way of quotation. When prayed quietly alone all the sentences and prayers are said. It is usually said in the morning, at noon, and in the evening, at the times when the Priest would be saying the Offices.

V/. The Angel of the Lord brought tidings unto Mary,

R/. And she conceived by the Holy Spirit.

Hail Mary full of grace, the Lord is with thee. Blessed art thou amongst women and blessed is the fruit of thy womb, Jesus. Holy Mary, Mother of God, pray for us sinners now and at the hour of our death. Amen.

V/. Behold the handmaid of the Lord.

R/. Be it unto me according to thy word.

Hail Mary.....

V/. And the word was made flesh,

R/. And dwelt among us.

Hail Mary......

V/. Let us pray.

Pour your grace into our hearts O Lord, and grant that as we have known the Incarnation of your Son, our Lord Jesus Christ, by the message of an angel, so by His cross ✟ and passion we may be brought unto the glory of His resurrection, through the same Christ our Lord. Amen.

(It is traditional for the sign of the cross to be made at ✟.)

Series 3

Some Holy Week Services Explained

14. Maundy or Holy Thursday

Maundy Thursday is usually observed with two great Eucharists: the Chrism Mass during the day, and the Mass of the Lord's Supper in the evening. This marks the beginning of the Easter Triduum, or three days in preparation for the Feast of Feasts: Easter. The Mass of the Lord's Supper is accompanied by other rites which dramatically, and powerfully, recreate the events and emotions of the Lord's last few hours of freedom, and his subsequent betrayal in the Garden of Gethsemane.

The Chrism Mass.
The Chrism Mass is the occasion when the Bishop makes the Holy Oils* used throughout the year. It is called the Chrism Mass because one of the three Holy Oils is called Chrism.

The Bishop gathers his clergy around him for this celebration, and very often they join with him in 'concelebrating'. This means they stand with him at the altar and join him in saying the words of the Eucharistic Prayer. In this way they exercise their common Priesthood. It is also the occasion when the clergy, both Priests and deacons, renew their vows and remind themselves of the high privilege and responsibility of their calling.

The Mass of the Lord's Supper.
The celebration falls into four parts:

1. The Mass itself followed by, 2. The solemn procession of the Blessed Sacrament to the Altar of Repose, followed by, 3. The Solemn Stripping of the altars, and finally followed by, 4. The

Watch until midnight. Within the context of the Mass there is often the ceremony of the Washing of Feet.

The Mass recreates the atmosphere and events in the Upper Room, when The Lord ate the Passover meal with His disciples before His betrayal by Judas. At that meal Our Lord gave His followers the commandment to love and serve one another, even if the cost is life itself. The word MAUNDY is derived from a French word, itself derived from a Latin word meaning 'commandment'. Our Lord expressed this commandment dramatically by stripping down to his loincloth and, with a towel tied around His waist, going to each of the disciples in turn, washing their feet; a job usually reserved for the lowest of the low of servants!

Where possible, after the homily, a number of men come to the front and take their shoes and socks off. The celebrating Priest takes his Chasuble** off and goes to each man in turn. He then pours water over their feet and dries them with a towel, just as Our Lord did! During this ceremony sentences called antiphons are sung which point up, and give a commentary on, the meaning of the action.

This was also the occasion on which Our Lord gave the Eucharist to the Church. This celebration, then, has the added dimension of being the principle act of thanksgiving for the gift of the Eucharist.

In The Garden.
After supper the Lord went with His disciples to the garden of Gethsemane to pray, and to await His betrayal. This event is portrayed liturgically and dramatically when Our Lord, in the form of the Blessed Sacrament, is taken by the Priest in Solemn Procession from the High Altar to a specially prepared and decorated side-chapel altar. This altar, called the Altar of Reposition or Repose, is often decorated with, and surrounded with, greenery to create the ambience of a garden. The Altar is also usually adorned

with very many candles as befits the Real Presence of the Lord. At the heart of the Altar a space is reserved for the Ciborium, or silver box, containing the Body of the Lord.

Desolate and abandoned.
After devotions at the Altar of Repose, the clergy and servers leave the laity to their prayers, and return to the main body of the Church. They then strip the Church and its altars of all its movable images and decorations. These include the altar frontals, cloths and hangings. This brings home to those present the sense of absolute dereliction and emptiness which those first disciples must have felt when their Lord was forcibly taken from them. It is also a reminder of what the world would be like without the Lord.

When this is finished, the Church remains in silence, and the laity are encouraged to spend some time watching in prayer with the Lord in the Garden. In practice people are encouraged to take part in a rota, to ensure that the Lord is never left unattended until midnight. At midnight the watch is ended, just as the disciples fled when Our Lord was arrested.

*. See chapter 2- Anointing with Oil' above.

**. A 'Chasuble' is the special tent-like coloured outer vestment worn by a Priest when celebrating the Eucharist.

15. Good Friday

The Celebration of the Lord's Passion.
We are taught that the celebration of the Lord's Passion takes place in the afternoon, about three o'clock', because it was at that time that the Lord suffered on the cross and died.

Next to the Easter celebration, which begins with the Vigil Mass on Holy Saturday night, this is the most important celebration in the Church's calendar, because there could have been no Resurrection without the cross.

On Good Friday, and Holy Saturday (before nightfall), the Church refrains from celebrating the sacraments, as she goes into mourning for the suffering and death of the Lord, and our part in it. She does, though, relive those events in the Liturgy of the Passion. This Liturgy falls into three parts: the Liturgy of the Word, the Proclamation of the Cross, and the Mass of the Presanctified (Holy Communion from the Reserved Sacrament).

The Setting.
In times past when one went into mourning, or wanted to express any deep sorrow, one would put off one's jewels, take-off one's makeup, wear dowdy or dark clothes, and generally make oneself uncomfortable. In the Bible we read of people showing their sorrow for sin by changing their comfortable clothes for rough sackcloth, and pouring ashes over their heads*.

On Good Friday the Church recognises its guilt and share of responsibility for the crucifixion. In response Christians are moved to fast as a sign of penitence and in solidarity with the suffering of the Lord. Outwardly the Church expresses its sorrow by stripping itself of ornamentation and beauty. Thus the Altar is stripped bare on

Maundy Thursday night, and left bare for the Good Friday celebration. All the movable statues, holy pictures, crosses and ornaments of the Church are also removed.

The Word.

The Priest, deacon, and servers enter the Church in silence wearing red vestments- the colour of blood! They bow before the Altar, then prostrate themselves on the floor, in complete submission and self-abasement.

The Liturgy of the Word follows, beginning with a prayer followed by readings from the Old and New Testaments. Then comes the reading of the Passion account according to St. John. Often the Passion is read by more than one person, in a dramatic way, which is designed to help the congregation to join-in emotionally as well as with their minds.

The Passion account is read, if possible my more than one person in a dramatic fashion, and is sometimes followed by a sermon, which is in turn followed by the general intercessions. These are often sung, and conform to a standard pattern. They consist of nine or ten intentions or prayers, depending upon whether the tradition of the Church is to pray for the Pope or not. The intentions are: 1. For the Church; 2. For the Pope; 3. For the clergy and laity; 4. For those preparing for baptism; 5. For the unity of Christians ; 6. For the Jewish people; 7. For those who do not believe in Christ; 8. For those who do not believe in God; 9. For all in public office; 10. For those in special need.

The Cross.

Having listened to the account of Christ's death, and pleaded that sacrifice for the needs of the Church and the world in the general intercessions, the congregation now dramatically relives the events of that first Good Friday. This liturgy can take one of two forms. In both cases a large crucifix is brought into Church by the deacon or Priest. Either the crucifix is covered with a veil and brought directly to the front of the Church or it is brought (uncovered) in a solemn procession from the back to the front of the church.

If the first form is used, the deacon or Priest uncovers the crucifix in three stages: first the upper part of it, second the right arm, finally the rest of it. At each point the cross is raised and shown to the people and the deacon or Priest sings 'This is the wood of the cross on which hung the Saviour of the world'. The people sing in response 'Come let us worship', then genuflect** as a sign of worship to God.

If the second form is used, the procession is like that of the Paschal Candle into Church at the Easter vigil. The deacon or Priest stops three times, and at each station raises the cross on high and sings as before 'This is the wood of the cross on which hung the Saviour of the world'. The people as before sing in response 'Come let us worship', then genuflect as a sign of worship to God.

Finally the cross is placed in front of the altar, where the clergy and people come forward to venerate it. This usually takes the form of a kiss.

Holy Communion.
After the Veneration of the Cross the Blessed Sacrament, which has been reserved on the Altar of Repose since the night before, is brought into Church and placed on the altar. The rite then continues with the Lord's Prayer, Holy Communion, and a final prayer. There is no final blessing, and Priest and people leave the Church in silence.

*. The rite of 'Ashing' on Ash Wednesday has a similar meaning. It recalls our minds to the effects of sin, when the Priest says 'remember that you are dust and unto dust you will return', while putting ashes onto our foreheads.

**. See Chapter 3- Genuflecting and Bowing.

16. Holy Saturday

A Drama in Four Acts.
Holy Saturday is the day before Easter Day. Holy Saturday night is the most important night in the Christian calendar, for it was during this night that the Lord rose again from the dead. As such it is celebrated with the most elaborate and moving liturgy imaginable. It is also the longest since it takes the form of a vigil, as the Church awaits the return of her Lord.

Act 1. Light shines in darkness; hope springs eternal.
Christ is called "the light of the world" by St. John in the fourth Gospel. On His death His Mother and His disciples must have felt the darkness to have returned with a vengeance. Their joy on learning of His resurrection sometime during the early hours of that Saturday night/Sunday morning would, therefore, have been all the more keenly felt. That joy is expressed in the liturgy of the New Fire, the consecration of the Paschal Candle and the solemn singing of the Exsultet or Easter Proclamation.

New Fire
Just as Light and warmth had left the world on Good Friday, its return is re-enacted dramatically by the kindling of a new fire outside the Church door. The flames of the new fire are blessed and the coals used for burning incense are ignited from the blessed fire.

The Paschal Candle
The Paschal Candle is the most potent symbol of Christ, the Light of The World. The candle is prepared by having certain holy signs engraved, or stuck onto it and traced by the hands of the Priest. The

symbols on the Paschal Candle are: a cross, the Alpha and Omega which are the first and last letters of the Greek alphabet and the numbers of the current year.

The symbolism of the cross needs no explanation. The Alpha and Omega are the first and last letters of the Greek alphabet, and are a title used for Christ in the last book of the Bible, the book of Revelation. The date is inscribed as the words of the prayer "all time belongs to him, and all the ages" are said. These symbols and words remind us that Christ is the beginning and the end of all things. Five grains of incense are also fixed to the cross representing the five wounds inflicted on Christ.

Once the Paschal Candle has been prepared the Priest says the words:

"May the light of Christ, rising in glory, dispel the darkness of our hearts and minds", as he lights the Candle from the new fire.

The Candle is then taken in solemn procession into the dark church, carried by the deacon or Priest. It is flanked by acolytes carrying unlit tapers and followed by the congregation each carrying an unlit candle. On its way to the front the procession stops three times. At each station the deacon or Priest turns to the people, raises the Candle high and sings: "Christ our light", to which the people respond: "Thanks be to God." At this point the people light their candles from the Paschal Candle, and so gradually the Church is flooded with light, which has its origins in the Paschal Candle!

The Exsultet.
This is the great Easter Proclamation which is sung by the Priest or deacon, by the light of the Paschal Candle and acolyte tapers.

Act 2. A word in time.

Seven readings are taken from the Old Testament, each of which is accompanied by a short prayer. The readings take us through the history of God's dealings with the Jewish people and with the world, focusing on God's preparations for the coming of Christ and His redeeming work.

After these readings the Gloria is sung to the accompaniment of bells which have remained silent throughout Lent. This is followed by the Reading from the Apostle Paul and the Gospel. Nine readings in all.

Act 3. The Liturgy of Baptism and renewal of Baptismal Vows.

This begins with a procession to the font in which the Priest carries the Paschal Candle. During the procession the Litany of The Saints is said or sung, in which many of the greatest saints are asked to pray for us. This is a timely reminder that the entire church, both on Earth and in heaven, shares in the joy of the resurrection and that it is united through the waters of Baptism.

At the font the Priest blesses the waters of Baptism, and by way of re-enactment lowers the Paschal Candle into the waters three times during the prayer. This is a reminder of the way in which Christ descended into the waters of death and re-emerged on the third day, death being unable to hold Him.

The Rite continues with the opportunity to renew our own Baptismal promises and rehearse the creed. Finally, our actual baptism is re-enacted as the Priest sprinkles the gathered congregation with the Holy Water. In the early Church this was the most important service in the year, for not only is it the first Mass of Easter but it was at this Mass that people were actually baptised.

Act 4. Liturgy of the Eucharist.

The Mass continues from the Offertory, and ends with the Solemn Blessing and singing of the great Easter Alleluias.

Series 4

Some Christian Ideas

17. Incarnation

Small fury animals are almost guaranteed to raise an "ooh!" of delight from small children, in much the same way as human babies seem designed to elicit "cooing" sounds from maternal women. Their apparent innocence, and helplessness, seems to bring out the best in so many people. Another by-product of these emotions is to encourage us to try to keep things as they are. How often has it been said, for example, "what a pity that they have to grow-up!"

For so many people Christmass is tied-up with all of these emotions and unspoken yearnings, writ large. It is all too often an excuse for a binge of nostalgia. Children have become the subjects of Christmass, and Christ the victim. Christ Himself is stripped of his manhood and has become little more than the universal baby, innocent, helpless, and unthreatening. He has been hedged about and enclosed in a womb from which there is no escape.

If the story of Christmass came to be written today it could well be the start of a heroic rags-to-riches saga. In fact Christmass is the beginning of a cave to cave story, for a womb is a kind of cave, and a cave became a kind of womb.

It is all too easy in our modern world to see the baby and overlook the God, yet both were there. The Almighty God who created the heavens and all they contain, the galaxies and the stars; who created the world and all it holds; who created the smallest atomic particle; who created the angels and archangels, and who created humanity, entered and allowed Himself to be constrained within a young woman's womb. That same God, the Son of the Almighty Father, was born in a cave, which doubled as a stable, and the representatives of creation came together to witness and wonder. The angels, the animals, the people, the star, all bore witness.

"Oh Figaro, look, look, the wishing star!

Star-light, star-bright, the first star I see tonight.

I wish I may, I wish I might, have the wish I make tonight!"

These famous words are spoken by the puppet-maker Giupetto, at the beginning of Walt Disney's classic Pinochio. Giupetto wished for a real boy, and his wish came true, but he would not have been the first or the last to make a wish; to wish upon a star.

Two thousand years ago the royal wise men, or Magi, did much the same thing. They were probably 'wise' in the ways of astrology, rather than astronomy, and felt able to interpret the sign of a new star in the heavens. Perhaps the star was a sign from God, indicating the birth of His Son as a man, or perhaps the voice of God was to be found in the unspoken wishes of the Magi, projected onto otherwise indifferent celestial phenomena. Perhaps the truth lies somewhere in between these two poles. Either way, the question remains as to what they wished for as they gazed up into the sky on that fateful night.

It is likely that the Magi wished for peace and prosperity, for themselves and for other people. They took with them gold as a gift for the Child, gold which is a symbol of worldly wealth, power and kingship. They hoped to find a King who would rule in wisdom and justice, and in this they represented the aspirations of all men. As with Giupetto, their wish was granted.

They also yearned to find God. Their souls must have thirsted for God, the living God, even as their bodies thirsted for water through the parched lands of the Arabian desert, and so they brought incense with which to worship. Their search for God was fuelled by the wish to fill the emptiness of their heathen souls. As with so many people today they longed to find a meaning in life, perhaps longed to find Life itself. As with Giupetto, their wish was granted.

The third gift brought by the Magi was Myrrh, and as with the other two it expressed their innermost desires. They sought a king, and they sought God, and finally they sought the bridge-builder between the two kingdoms, a High Priest. What they found was the Priest King, of the order of Melchizedek, and they brought the myrrh oil with which to anoint him, and proclaim Him. As with Giupetto, their wish was granted. The full significance of their action, though, could not have been clear to them, for their choice of myrrh was also prophetic. The myrrh they brought foreshadowed not only the priest, but the victim, for it pointed towards Christ's death and burial. Myrrh mixed with wine was given to Our Lord on the cross, it was also used to embalm His lifeless corpse for the tomb.

The Magi followed a star, and found a Star, Christ who is the Morning Star which never sets. When we gaze upon that Morning Star and wish-pray, the desires of our hearts are revealed. They are revealed for all to see, although we ourselves are all too often the last to see. They are discovered by the way we put our prayer into action. Perhaps our secret prayer, not the one we would admit to, is for worldly wealth, power, and kingship...for ourselves. Perhaps it is for glory...for ourselves. Or perhaps, like the Magi, we come in humility, searching for God, for His sake. If so we, like the Magi, shall surely find the object of our desires.

St. John tells us that "the Word became flesh and dwelt among us." These words are at the heart of the Christian faith. They describe the new relationship between God and Man. The relationship created in Christ, which is summed-up in the word Incarnation.

It is impossible for us to 'picture' God, the God who made everything from the smallest atom to the largest galaxy; He is so great that our imaginings can never 'do Him justice'. That is why, in the first of the Ten Commandments, we were forbidden to "make any graven image" of Him, in case we were tempted to cut God down to our own size! On the other hand we are told that we are made in His image, yet however much we try, we can never live up to that description of ourselves.

In spite of these problems, impossible for us to overcome, God wants us to know and love Him. Since we cannot find Him, however hard we try, God has revealed Himself to us, over and over again! In the Old Testament we can read the story of God's attempts to show Himself to the world through the prophets, and through His dealings with the Jewish people. In all of this God was preparing for the time when He would not only show us what He is like, but show us Himself!

Most people, at one time or another, have felt sympathy for another person. Sometimes this feeling is impersonal, and for people whom we have never known. Sometimes we feel for people who are very close to us. Sympathy enables us to get alongside the other person/people by imagining what they might be experiencing, but it does not enable us to truly share their suffering. Neither does sympathy give the other person confidence that we can do anything about their problem! What is required is empathy, not merely imagination, not merely walking alongside, but personal experience which enables us to step into their shoes.

God has shown us Himself by stepping into our shoes. He did this by enabling a man to live-up to the description 'made in the image of God'. Jesus could only be the 'perfect' Man, though, if He was also the pattern on which Man was modelled: God Himself.

The world is rather like an artist's painting, the artist being God. To the tutored eye the subtle differences of brush-technique, use of colour, style and the like is often enough to reveal the identity of the artist. To most of us, though, and even to the expert, the most important indication is the signature of the artist. The signature of God is all the goodness and beauty we see around us. Of all of God's creations, however, His masterpiece is Mankind. We are no mere landscape or still-life, "God created Man in His own image"; we are God's self-portrait! There is no need of subtle techniques to identify the artist, nor even of a signature. What is needed is some acquaintance with the artist Himself!

The problem lies in what has been done to the painting. All too often the image has been so scored, creased, and generally defaced, that the original portrait has become all-but unrecognisable. The reality of God the Father can then only be clearly perceived in the works and Person of God the Son, for God the Son is the extension of God the Father into our knowable world. Thus a bridge is established between the unknowable and 'immutable', or changeless and self-sufficient God, and the world which is His creation.

A helpful metaphor might be that of a hologram, or three dimensional image, where the two dimensional original is hidden from view. It is only by extending itself into three dimensions that the two-dimensional original can be apprehended. This does not mean that God the Father in Himself lacks anything, nor that the Father and the Son are indistinguishable, rather, that the Father cannot possibly be seen apart from the Son.

It is only in the person of Christ that we see God's BEING expressed clearly. Without the Son or 'Word' there would be no link between the unknowable God and the world. In fact without the Son there would be no world, for the world does not co-exist with God. It is totally dependent upon God's continuing creative activity. God's creativity, in turn, is dependent upon His 'ability' to effect change without Himself being changed. Without the 'Word' the BEING of God would have no means of doing anything whilst remaining unmoved and changeless. In sharing a human life and death, and rising from the grave, God has shown us Himself without being compromised. He has also repaired the relationship between Mankind and Himself and, what is more, He has opened a door for us which would have been unthinkable before. In the Incarnation of Christ, God and Man were united, never again to be separated and Man has been perfected in God's image.

Many Christians tend to think of the Incarnation solely in terms of the earthly ministry of Christ, but in doing so they are seriously mistaken. St. Paul describes the Church as the Body of Christ, with Christ Himself as the head. As a metaphor this expresses the Truth that the Incarnation has not come to an end, but rather has been perpetuated and extended in the Church, corporately and in the lives of individual Christians, by virtue of their incorporation into the Church. In taking His inclusive Manhood with Him when He ascended, He permits us to share in the eternal life of God!

The first man in outer space was the Russian cosmonaut Yuri Gagarin. In those days Russia was ruled by Marxist communists, who believe that there is no God. Although Yuri Gagarin's space flight was a great human achievement, it was marred by being used for propaganda purposes. One of the first things which Gagarin said was along the lines of: "well, I'm up here and I can't see God anywhere!"

It is not only communists who think like that; a great many Christians, including some theologians, think along the same lines. They believe that since God is clearly not "up there" in the sky, Christ cannot have ascended into heaven, and so the story must be untrue or misleading. The truth is that Christ not only did ascend, but had to ascend to His Father in heaven. This does not mean, however, that 'heaven' is a place somewhere in the sky.

Arguably one of the most enduring images on film is that of the Western hero, having done his good deeds, riding-off into the distance. This kind of ending leaves the viewer 'hanging', hoping for more. The image encourages the imagination to believe that the hero has not actually left, but has merely moved to another part of our world. One is almost tempted to believe that if one went-off in search of him, sooner or later one would find him. On the other hand the image of somebody rising into the air and disappearing is the most powerful symbol of leaving this world altogether.

The sense of finality is etched into the consciousness of the witnesses in a way that no other leave-taking could have achieved. It emphasised the futility of searching for "the living amongst the dead" (Luke ch24 v5)! The Ascension, though, was no mere symbol. It happened, for only by returning to His Father, taking His Manhood with Him and thus continuing the Incarnation, could He keep open the door to heaven.

The means whereby the Incarnation is extended into the Church is through the Sacraments. In the Sacrament of the Eucharist the extension of the Incarnation into the Church is seen most clearly. God takes the ordinary things of this world, in this case bread and wine, and makes of them the extraordinary means of His real presence, objectively, amongst us.

Christ promised that the bread would become His flesh, and the wine His blood, and as with all living people His presence is inseparable from the presence of His living body. The miracle of the Incarnation is brought into the midst of the Church each time the priest utters the words of Christ with the intention that Christ's promise be fulfilled.

It is worthy of note that when Christ said those words, and spoke of recalling Himself into our present, He had not yet died, and it must therefore be the Incarnate Christ which is recalled for His promise to be kept and intelligible! Since there is only one Christ, who makes Himself present amongst us in and through the Eucharistic elements, the Risen and Ascended Christ must also be the Incarnate Christ.

The Book of Common Prayer defines sacraments as "effectual signs of grace", in much the same way as a smile is an outward and visible sign of happiness. A smile not only reflects one's mood, but contributes to creating that mood, in the person concerned, and in those around him. Sacraments work in a similar way. The Sacraments of the Church both demonstrate symbolically what God does through them, and are the very means whereby God achieves the demonstrated effect.

A useful image is that of a reservoir high-up in the hills. Such a reservoir is like God, in that without its water the crops in the valley fields would fail and there could be no life. The problem is in getting the water from the reservoir to the valley. This is achieved by providing, in this case, seven channels or canals from the reservoir to the valley: the seven Sacraments. By means of these seven Sacraments Christ provides for all the possible needs of the Church, and through them guarantees the present active power of the Holy Spirit. This is not to say that God confines Himself to the Sacraments, but that only in the Sacraments does He guarantee His presence. In and through the Sacraments Christ is united with His Church, and thus with the World, with an intimacy only to be found elsewhere in the union of a Bride and Groom.

In the Gospel according to St. John, Our Lord tells Nicodemus that in order for a man to enter the Kingdom of Heaven it is necessary for him to be born again of water and the spirit. This is exactly what happens when a person is baptised. Just as the two sides of Christ's nature, or rather His two natures, cannot be separated, neither can the two components of Baptism be separated. A person cannot be 'baptised in the Spirit', without the accompanying rite of baptism in water, any more than could the Son of God also have become the Son of Man without first entering into the Virgin's womb and taking flesh of her flesh.

Each time a person is baptised, be he child or adult, the miracle of the Incarnation is once again witnessed. It is not without reason that Eastern Orthodox Christians talk of the Deification of men: the re-making of men into God, by adoption! The Eucharist and Baptism are only two of the seven sacraments of the Church, albeit the two most important, but in and through them all the Incarnation is expressed and extended. They are the channels through which He delivers, or imparts, the effects of His life, death and resurrection; and the power which enables the Sacraments? The Holy Spirit, as He was the Power which brought about the conception of the Lord and His Incarnation in the first place.

18. Resurrection

A notorious incident in the First 'Gulf War' demonstrated one of the most enduring problems of warfare, that of 'recognition'; how to distinguish friend from foe. In the past all kinds of tricks were employed to make recognition easier; for example, flags were flown and coats of arms were emblazoned on shields. In the Gulf War, fought mainly from the air on the allied side, easy recognition was important as never before. The 'Friendly Fire' incident, in which several British soldiers died from an American airstrike on their tanks, was an illustration of the importance of effective recognition. After the event the American pilots involved asserted that the British tanks had failed to display the appropriate symbols, whereas the British authorities were adamant that they had. Whatever the cause, however, the pilots had failed to recognise their allies, with disastrous consequences.

The need for effective recognition, and the hazards which may accompany failure, are not confined to warfare. Everyday life is full of examples. How difficult it sometimes is to recognise somebody whose appearance has been changed, whether by accident or design, by having a 'blue-rinse' or growing a beard perhaps; and having failed to recognise, how embarrassing or even hurtful the result!

The priest's clerical collar is the perfect illustration of the problem. For much of his life the priest wears his 'uniform', the clerical collar, and only occasionally will he be seen without it around his parish or perhaps beyond. On those occasions, though, he can so easily go unrecognised by many of his parishioners, even perhaps by some who know him quite well. While sitting on a train or in a pub engaged in conversation with a stranger, the interesting part comes when, albeit rarely, the stranger eventually becomes aware of the identity of the priest! Physical appearance, though, is not wholly dependent upon external factors such as clothing and make-up. It is often affected or even altered by internal factors such as the way we feel, or the way our personalities have changed as a result of life-experiences or simple ageing.

A quite common experience is that of meeting an old friend or acquaintance after a lapse of many years. The traumas of life may well have left their mark in the form of deep furrows, perhaps a thoughtful depth to the eyes, and in a thousand other ways. Initially one may have no idea that one ever knew the other person, but as the conversation continues the truth begins to dawn. Whether it dawns gradually, or explodes in an instant, recognition often comes with a shock, and the key may not have been the person's appearance. The trigger may have been either something the other person said, or even in the way they said it, or a physical mannerism. Perhaps it was the way he/she brushed the hair from their eyes that did it, or maybe something even simpler! Physical appearance, then, is the first and perhaps the most noticeable element in the recognition of people, but it is not the only element; our words and mannerisms are just as important to correct recognition as our appearance.

Christ, the Son of God, was also the Son of Man, and as such was as easy or as difficult to recognise as the rest of us. As with all of us, the same three elements were operative in the process of recognition, a fact both understood and utilised by Our Lord, yet so often overlooked by certain modern commentators on the New Testament.

Christ did not look divine. He was not of superhuman appearance, he did not sport a glowing halo at a jaunty angle, and bolts of lightning did not flash from his eyes frying his enemies at a glance. On the contrary, to all intents and purposes he was indistinguishable from his contemporaries; even his behaviour was largely unremarkable until he began his ministry, unlike John the Baptist, and then he was noted not for piety but for apparent irreverence! It is hardly surprising then that few people were able to recognise in the Jesus of Nazareth, the Christ, the Son of God. Even His closest followers remained ignorant of His true identity for most of their time with Him, as attested by their reaction to the miracle of the Stilling of the Storm: "Who is this that even the winds and the waves obey him?" It was only towards the close of His earthly ministry that the truth began to dawn.

"Jesus said 'who do men say that the Son of Man is?' And they said, 'some say John the Baptist, others say Elijah, and others say Jeremiah or one of the prophets.' He said to them, 'But who do you say that I am?' Simon Peter replied, 'You are the Christ, the Son of the Living God.' And Jesus answered him, 'Blessed are you Simon Bar-Jona! For flesh and blood have not revealed this to you, but my Father who is in heaven."

What had given Peter the clue? Surely it was the things that Jesus said, and the way in which He said them, coupled to the things He did, and the way He did them. We are told, for example, that people were impressed by His teaching because He taught with authority, not like their regular teachers and leaders. Similarly His works were signs of power, not merely echoing the ancient prophecies or hinting at their fulfilment, but dramatizing them. There was nothing low-key about the way Christ went about His business. Even so, in the end still only a few people recognised Him, and that was by design.

At the very beginning of His ministry Christ was given the opportunity to choose his path, in the desert. 'Bedazzle and bully with mighty acts of unmistakable power; show yourself openly to be what you are, and the world will be at your feet' comes one temptation, amongst others. But the result would not be love or faith, devotion freely given; instead life's futility would be reinforced by endless tyranny, ruled over by God the puppet-master, a divine Fuhrer. Christ rejected that path, and chose instead the gentle way which alone could guarantee, for those who responded, a share in His victory. The cost of recognition for some was then, and remains today, the freedom permitted the rest to deny Him, and ultimately to remain lifeless and hopeless; the pain of which continues to rend Christ's sacred heart.

Recognition was no less a problem after the Resurrection than it was before, if anything it is highlighted in the accounts of His appearances and in recent years has given rise to doubts concerning the nature and reality of the Resurrection. Opinion is divided broadly between those for whom the Resurrection is no more than a 'faith' experience, by which seems to be meant that it did not really happen, and those for whom it was a physical event which subsequently gave rise to the response of faith.

For the sceptics there is no need of a physical event, for Christ is alive in 'the spirit'. There are too many inconsistencies in the Resurrection accounts for them to be given any real credence. At the heart of all the inconsistencies is the inability of many of the witnesses to recognise The Lord, some at least of whom would have been expected to recognise The Lord instantly. Secondly, it is pointed out that in at least one account The Lord is physically solid, whilst in at least one other account He apparently has the ability to pass through walls and locked doors. Too many impossibilities and inconsistencies, argue the sceptics, for the accounts to be believed, at least at face value.

They have a point! Even St. Paul is compelled to address the problem in his first letter to the Corinthians 15:35ff: "But some will ask, 'How are the dead raised? With what kind of body do they come?'" The main difference between the modern sceptics and St. Paul seems to be that although the sceptics appear to view Christ's Resurrection in similar terms to those employed by modern Spiritualists, as an immaterial event at best, St. Paul quite clearly does not. He uses the term 'spiritual body' to denote a 'glorified' extension of the earthly, material body of Christ. By the careful use of metaphors, notably that of the seed and wheat, he emphasises the continuity of the imperishable body with the perishable. A merely subjective 'faith experience', albeit individual or group, together with an immaterial phantasmal body are clearly far from St. Paul's mind. What are we left with?

The inescapable impression left by St. Paul and the Evangelists is one of continuity coupled with change. It is remarkable that in spite of the differences in style and theological approach, the evangelists all record the inconsistencies, with no apparent effort to iron them out, on its own a fact which tends to support the historical accuracy of the records. The problem, then, is to understand the inconsistencies without stretching the bounds of credulity. One possible explanation, which eliminates the need to 'de-mythologise' the Resurrection accounts consists of two strands.

Firstly, even as human appearance may be effectively altered by life-experience and trauma, it is that much more likely that Christ's appearance will have been affected by His experiences. Christ was subjected to the most brutal kinds of torture and death, but unlike any human before or since He also had to endure descent into hell, and then Resurrection. Such trauma would have been unimaginably profound and cannot have failed to have left its mark in His appearance. It is hardly surprising that He was difficult to recognise.

The analogy of the caterpillar and the butterfly may prove helpful. There is no doubt a traceable continuity between the caterpillar and the butterfly, albeit that the butterfly exhibits remarkably different abilities to the caterpillar. Different in appearance and abilities, the two are actually the same creature. Christ's glorified resurrected body was no mere resuscitated corpse. The relationship between the two was no doubt complex, but that the latter was based on the former seems incontrovertible. Many sceptics would argue that such inconsistencies as Christ being both physically solid and yet able to penetrate walls and pass through walls are insurmountable. One does not have to be a Biblical Fundamentalist, though, to believe that the same Christ who had authority and power to order, and re-order, the very laws of nature before His death would have retained and amplified such abilities after His Resurrection.

Secondly, there is every reason to suppose that God's purposes remained unchanged, which alone would account for the differing ways in which the fact of the Resurrection was revealed to various witnesses. As with all the other miracles of Christ, the principal significance of which lay in the response of faith they were designed to elicit, the Resurrection was presented to each of the witnesses in such a way as to elicit the response appropriate to each. God's purpose was not merely to demonstrate that He was capable of performing a feat of power, but to enable the witnesses to respond from the heart; not merely to recognise, but to believe.

In each case, then, recognition occurs on a different level. St. Thomas, unable to respond at a deeper level, is presented with a greater degree of continuity than, for example, St. Peter. For St. Thomas the resurrected Christ, to be the same as the Christ that had been crucified would have to be recognisably the same body, exhibiting the wounds and capable of many of the same things. The fact that St. Peter recognised the Lord in response to what He did and said, rather than His appearance, cannot be taken to imply either that he or St. Thomas were mistaken, or that one or other of the accounts is historically inaccurate. Nor can it be taken to imply that he was dealing with a 'ghost', or inner feeling, or mass 'hallucination', however the idea may be dressed-up and made to look respectable. Rather that the Lord's intention was more than simply to show Himself.

When He appeared to Mary immediately after the Resurrection in the Garden, we are not told whether His appearance was altered or not. The fact is of no importance since it would have been too dark to matter. What is of significance is that He was recognisable, by the way in which He said her name. She was not talking to herself, any more than she was rationalising the way in which she felt or was hallucinating.

None of the apostles easily recognised Our Lord when He appeared to them at the lakeside, nonetheless He was considerably more than a mere apparition, capable of cooking and eating a meal with them. He was no more recognisable than Moses would have been recognisable when he descended from the mountain, but He was the same person, possessing an objective reality; still the Son of Man as well as the Son of God.

Then there is the appearance to the disciples on the road to Emmaus to consider. In this instance, they spent some time in the company of The Lord without recognising Him. Only after the event did they conclude that they had known all along that it had been He; clearly an attempt at rationalisation. This is such a human touch, bearing the hallmark of honesty in the face of difficulty, that the veracity of the record, and the historicity of the event, is put beyond doubt. Again, though, the incident cannot be taken to throw doubt upon the objective reality and the continuity of the Risen Christ with the crucified Lord. Rather that The Lord's purpose in appearing in this way was more than to demonstrate His power, or even to empirically prove His survival , albeit that He achieved both these ends as well. In both incidents one of His primary purposes appears to have been to elicit the response of faith, a faith grounded in an objective reality.

To say that one believes in 'Christ's Resurrection', but that one does not believe it was in any way a 'physical' resurrection, is to beg the question as to how one's belief differs from that of, for example, modern spiritualists. They, along with members of many other sects, claim to believe in the universal survival of human personality after death. They believe that the vehicle of human expression continues to be a kind of immaterial, or astral, body. Why should their claims be any less respectable, and likely, than those made for the resurrection of Jesus, if there is little or no tangible difference between them, except in the mind of the believer? On the other hand, the claims made for Christ's resurrection have, from the earliest days of the Church, distinguished it from all doctrines. It differs fundamentally in that it affirms the value of human existence in this world, by demonstrating the glorification of humanity in the next and beyond. Christ's physical resurrection, no less than the Son of God's Incarnation, or becoming a full human being, was an essential part of God's plan for the redemption of the world, and remains an essential article of Christian faith.

Made in the USA
Charleston, SC
09 May 2016